INTRODUCTION

"For I know the plans I have for you, says the Lord. They are plans for good and not for disaster, to give you a future and a hope."
~Jeremiah 29:11

If you're here, I'm excited for both of us. For you because I pray my words set your soul on fire. That they put a beat in your heart to know the person reading them is so deeply loved. That every chapter brings you to an understanding of the beauty that Christ designed when you were created. A knowledge in the fact that every scripture verse you take in, was done so that you understand that no matter how dark the pit, how big the wrong, how far you think you are running, God is with you.

For me, because this was my journey. My understanding of what loving and being loved by Christ really means. It's a journal of my heart. A pile of words that show just how mighty God has moved in my life. My truth. My Dear Denise....it all turned out alright.

DEDICATION

To the beauty struggling with her truth. He found you. He
loves you.
You are the Beloved. You are salt and light.
You are not alone. You have been redeemed.

'DON'T LET THE WORLD DEFINE YOUR SPARKLE!'

"For we are God's masterpiece. He has created us anew in Christ Jesus, so we can do the good things He planned for us long ago." Ephesians 2:10

*D*ear Daughter looking for her shine,
      Daughter of the Most High God. That is your real name. Did you know that? Our perfect heavenly Father knit you together in your mother's womb before anyone knew you existed.

Almost every woman is familiar with that little voice that nags you about your appearance. You know who I'm talking about. From the moment you are born, this world has tried to define and mold you. None of it has been, or will be, true. That voice has been there since the moment you realized your appearance mattered.

Sometimes that voice is still, other times it's screaming and roaring.

The moment you spotted someone else with perfect hair, dazzling makeup or an outfit that looked like it was made just for her, and you felt that clutch in your stomach? That was the little voice getting started, reminding you of everything you're not. The little voice took hold the moment you realized that this world valued the outer beauty way more than the shine coming from the inside, that voice was there.

The moment that my ugly, little voice entered is distinct and used to play on repeat in my head like a song that just wouldn't go away.

~

I was six years old sitting in the balcony of First Baptist Church of Lewisville, Texas. I was a young girl brand new in my salvation and starting my walk with Jesus alone.

My mother had gotten me up like she did many Sundays before, got me ready and put me on the bus to church. It was the first time I had ever been a part of the large service. I had previously only attended Sunday school, and it was held separate from the main service. The only other memories I have to compare this moment to are the sporadic images of holding onto my late grand-father's hand as we sat in stiff high back pews in a cold church in Detroit. I sat pretty and smiling, because that is what little girls do.

This particular Sunday we sat up high. Every dark blue cloth covered pew was jammed packed. My little heart beat fast with excitement. A real church service! This is what the adults did on Sunday, the ones who grew up to love the Jesus I was learning about. Then I heard it: "Ugh! Why do we have to sit up here! These are the bus kids, the ones who smell funny, and wear cheap church clothes. Their parents aren't even here." Her mother gave a polite smile and quickly shuffled her up higher.

~

I never knew that little girl's name, but I let her define me and my walk with Jesus for a very long time.

I let her dim my shine.

If only.

If only I had sought the Lord at that very moment.

If only I had thicker skin, if only...

But I didn't.

I let that little girl change my view of "church", and how to love those around me.

I spent many, many years after that fighting to no longer being labeled that "bus girl".

I slipped on a mask, and instead of being molded into the child of God He wanted me to be, I became the face that the world suggested I be. The right hair, clothes, speech, and weight. I would make poor decisions, hurt others, and damage relationships on my way to reach these goals that I let that little girl set for me. The entire time I was walking further and further away from God's original ordainment as His precious daughter.

The Lord knew that I would carry these mountains of a stumbling block that could only be conquered by finding my value and worth in Him. Christ lives in you, let Him shine, let the world know that He is the only definition that you will go by. Stay rooted in Him, because His view of your self-worth is beyond measure and comparison that anyone else could make.

"Let your roots grow down into him, and let your lives be built on him." ~Colossians 2:7

*T*ake a breath and realize the stronger your foundation is built on Him, the better you will be able to recognize His truth and not the world's lies. When you are covered in His truth and love, you can walk in a light that can never be put out.

Sparkle on,
Your (mask-less) Sister in Christ
Denise

*S*tudy Questions:

1. What moment in your life negatively impacted the

way you view yourself? Does it still effect you today?

2. Write down three ways that you would describe your personality to someone else.

3. Take the time this week to memorize scripture that reminds you who you are as the daughter of the King. (If you are struggling, here are a few to get you started)

"We are therefore Christ's ambassadors, as though God were making his appeal through us. We implore you on Christ's behalf: Be reconciled to God."
2 Corinthians 5:20
"Therefore, if anyone is in Christ, the new creation has come: The old is gone, the new is here!" 2 Corinthians 5:17
"In Him we were also chosen, having been predestined according to the plan of Him who works out everything in conformity with the purpose of His will."
Ephesians 1:11

PERFECTLY IMPERFECT...JUST THE WAY GOD INTENDED

*"So, God created mankind in his own image, in the image of
God he created them; male and female he created them."-
Genesis 1:28*

*D*ear daughter holding judgement for herself,
My body is a road map of life.

Those stretch marks are the roads to childbirth, too much comfort found in food and the glory of a 6'ft tall body of an Amazon. The cellulite, scars, crooked tooth, too short lashes, and tummy pouch are all a blessing and part of the beautiful creation that God labeled me. I know you just envisioned all of this in your head, and it's a mess. But God finds it absolutely amazing. So, will I. So, do I.

~

"She is clothed with strength and dignity,and she laughs without fear of the future. When she speaks, her words are wise, and she gives instructions with kindness and she gives instructions with kindness.Proverbs 31:25-26

~

*G*irlfriend embrace it (with modesty!) and love who you are created to be. The world will define you. Everywhere we turn the world is going to tell you how to be, how to dress, how much you should or shouldn't weigh. The sad truth, they are looking for, and defining things they have no true knowledge of. They plaster altered images of celebrities and things that have no stake in the beauty that is you. Did you catch that word? *Altered.* Even the images we subscribe too as truth have been altered.

Those stars and flowers you admire in nature?

The God of the universe made those things and He made you with the same beauty in mind. Your beauty was created by the most high for a purpose, from love.

Stop chasing numbers on a scale. Stop looking at altered

images and believing that's what you should look like. There is only one you. God looks down on His masterpiece and is so very proud. You are His imagine. If you hold Him in awe, why can't you glimpse that in the image you see reflecting back in the mirror?

No man, no pill, no amount of likes on ' the gram' is going to place in you the love God holds for you.

Can you just imagine the love and care He had when forming you?

You're going to be okay. You have to stop being so hard on yourself. Those goals won't happen till God is viewed as the Master of Design, who created the beauty that is you.

Find a mirror and thank God for every imperfection, because it makes you unique.

There isn't much more I can say to you here. You have to grasp the concept that God loves all of you. You have to let the world know that you are more than a number on the scale, that no amount of filters or airbrushing is going to cover up the things you need to let God heal. So, let's start there.

At my absolute heaviest I hit 456 on the scale. In 5 I've shed 200 of those pounds. I'm healthy and happy in this place and in this moment. You know why? I let God love me, I prayed and asked Him "years,Show me what you see."

The world still judges me. Sometimes I let it get to me. But on those hard days I'm constantly reminded how truly loved and beautiful God finds me.

Sparkle on,
Your (beautiful) Sister in Christ
Denise

~

*S*tudy Questions

1) What will it take to make you feel beautiful? Was God the first thing that came to mind? If not, what steps can you take to change that view?

2) What moment in your life negatively impacted the way your view yourself? Does it still effect you today?

3) Write down three ways that you would describe your personality to someone else. Do you see God shining through in those areas? How can you make sure you are using this to work in ministry?

4) What are some words, scripture, or advice you would use to encourage someone that might be dealing with self-image issues?

'WORSHIP LIKE NO ONE IS WATCHING!'

*"Singing psalms and hymns and spiritual songs among
yourselves, and making music to the Lord in your hearts."
Ephesians 5:19*

ear daughter longing for a closer relationship with God,

Let me just share a little something about myself here, I speak in song lyrics. I can turn any word or statement into some kind of song reference. All these most often useless lyrics just rolling around in my head. I know a really lame superpower. The flip side of this, worship songs. Lyrics that seem to float in my head just when I need a reminder. Just when I'm having a hard moment and need a reminder of HIM.

So why worship?

Why is this so important?

Because our hearts long for it, we crave it.

Nothing but joy, peace, and a closeness to God can define this experience.

It's a crying out of our souls, a moment with Abba (our God the Father), a place of rest. This is a moment of thanks for things we will never be worthy of. It's a battle cry, a reminder.

In a worldly definition we have made when people speak of worship:

to idolize,

to adore,

to hold in reverence.

In many ways these things are right. But let's put this all into perspective. We worship athletes, musicians, movie stars, our possessions. We've watered down this word, this moment.

Can I be honest here?

I really struggled writing this chapter.

Let's call it inspiration. Because I spent many hours in prayer, with my favorite Christian songs on repeat to get to a place where I could express to you guys how very important these moments are.

I needed a moment to truly understand what it means to worship God the Father.

Some moments of worship are loud, rumbling, feet stomping, hands flying, voices raised. And those moments rock.

But you know the moments that get me?

Those silent moments of worship.

Sitting in a chair, having a conversation with God and thanking Him for things I know I will never be worthy of, but that He chooses for me anyway.

Is this why we struggle? Why we find it difficult to thank God for things we know we are not worthy of?

Please take heart this is not meant to be a moment of condemnation for you. This is a moment for you to soak in the simple sum, that though we aren't worthy, He has given it to us anyway. I need you beautiful souls to mark out time in your days for this. If you don't,, you will start to get a world view of things you "deserve" and "should" have. You will begin to forget that you are worthy of endless love, because He choose to become broken and torn apart to save you.

∼

"But I, by your great love, can come into your house;
in reverence I bow down toward your holy temple."
Psalm 5:7

∼

Come to the Fathers house. Worship at His feet.
Let your soul be renewed, rested.
Listen to the sweet things He will whisper in your ear.
Delight in His truths.

Dance, shout, raise your hands.

Love, love. love.

Give thanks.

It sets the tone for your day and it gives you fuel to get through the day. It balances out the noise of this world. Worship, because it will be your battle cry in the face of the enemy.

Sparkle on,
Your Sister, Dancing in Christ's Glory
Denise

tudy Questions

1. When you see the word worship, what does it mean to you?
2. What things are holding you back from fully worshiping God when you've committed time to it?
3. How can you change the things that hold you back?
4. What are some things you would like to change about how you worship?
5. Write down your 3 favorite worship songs.

'THAT FOUNDATION NEEDS SOME EXTRA GLUE... AND GLITTER.'

"Together, we are His house, built on the foundation of the apostles and the prophets. And the cornerstone is Christ Jesus himself." Ephesians 2:20

*D*ear Daughter trying to figure out why life is constantly shaking you,

If our faith is our foundation, and that faith is found in Christ, why do we find ourselves crumbling the minute we spill our coffee?

This often times is an all true statement for me. A truth I constantly battle to let go.

If your foundation is built on anything but Christ, it will fall the minute it's put to the test.

Do you trust Him? I mean really TRUST.

If you were walking down the road, would you stop to look at a random burning bush and think it was utter nonsense to hear a voice tell you it was from God. Would you obey if you lost your new husband and were in a place where you only had your mother-in-law to lean on? Would you have faith if you were told to have a baby out of wedlock who was going to save the world?

These aren't headlines from the tabloids, these are words our Father wanted us to see, read, soak in, meditate on.

Life changing, earth rocking, foundation setting events.

Do you trust HIM?

What if His response to your questioning, was I AM WHO I AM?

Still following?

I can't tell you what it's going to take to bring you here. There have been so many occasions in my life where I'm brought back to this line of questioning. Time where things are going a little to well and God sees fit to rock me, to remove me from that comfortable perch. Because though He put me there, I forgot Him. I stopped leaning on Him, and ran to the world for comfort and answers. Then in those moments of crying in pain and frustration I'll hear it. " Lean not on your own understand….."

Have you ever looked back on a situation, and realized that God had laid out every single thing to see you through? The people, the answers, the moments when you didn't know how you were going to continue but God showed up, and showed up BiG. Bills paid, meals stretched out just enough, No's become Yes's, lost things restored.

Ya'll that was Jesus!!!

∾

"Early in the morning, as Jesus was on his way back to the city, he was hungry. Seeing a fig tree by the road, he went up to it but found nothing on it execpt leaves. Then he said to it, "May you never bear fruit again!" Immediately the tree withered. When the disciples saw this, they were amazed. "How did the fig tree wither so quickly?" they asked. Jesus replied, "Truly I tell you, if you have faith and don't doubt, not only can you do what was done to the fig tree, but you can say to a mountain, 'Go, throw yourself into the sea,' and it will be done. If you believe, you will receive what you ask for in prayer."
Matthew 21:18-22

∾

*B*elief in HIM, belief in the power that He has given you, placed upon you when you gave Him your heart. That is your foundation. That is the thing that will hold you when the world tries to break you. Let the cracks of your foundation be purified in and turned to gold.

Loves you need to understand, that God wants nothing but the very best for you.Please don't take this statement to mean, you will have everything your heart desires, because honey, this battle is not about us. Our savior was a carpenter who rode into a city at his peak of "fame" on a donkey. James declares in the opening of scripture, "Count it all Joy, these trials and tribulations…" At this very moment and my strongest walk with God to date in my 37 years, I've battled cancer, been a survivor of rape, healed from abusive situations, and had to count pennies to feed my family. My saviour redeems it all, but in this walk, I will count it all JOY! He delights in your joy. But you have to trust the things He hands you, even when you don't know the plan. Look how Job suffered. In the end he never knew why, but God restored, and blessed His child ten fold. I don't know about you, but that's the kind of faith I want my foundation built on. His word, and His promise. In this life, this world, it is the only thing that won't fail you.

Before we dive into the questions at the end of this chapter, here is a little something to spend time contemplating. Do things we set our sights on, the foundations of what we spend our time, and daily lives doing, does it fall in line with God?

Do not doubt that God won't speak to you about your path. Where He wants you to be. He will speak to you through fellow believers, in your prayer time, in your dreams at night. Pray! Ask Him to show you where your foundation needs some God glitter.

Sparkle on,
Your Sister, firmly in Christ
Denise

*S*tudy Questions

1. What experiences in your life would you call "foundation rocking"?

2. How did God see you through those experiences?
3. Are there doubts that you need to cast? List them here, then cross them out.
4. Write down at least 3 things that you need to faithfully lay at God's feet. Continue to pray over them, write down when you see a change.

'WHERE'S THAT FANCY CAR AND MY NAME IN LIGHTS?'

"Humble yourselves under the mighty power of God, and at the right time He will lift you up in honor." 1 Peter 5:6

ear Daughter sitting in a pile of disappointment,
Oh bless your heart!

You drank the tea, and swallowed that Pinterest pill.

Now don't get me wrong, your girl could waste a day on Pinterest.

The keyword there is… waste.

God has got to be enough.

Sitting on the newest trending couch, sipping out of the new cute coffee mug, while scrolling through the latest DIY trends, is never going to fulfill you.

It's a big old stumbling block to the design God has for your life.

Let me make this very clear and shout it extra loud for the people in the back…

Nowhere in God's word are we promised earthly riches and glory in His name.

No. Where.

Certainties, unconditional love, freedom, peace, an eternity with the one who loves us more than anyone ever can or will…. how do we gain these things?

By simply calling on God.

Holding onto faith, and knowing His plan and will are greater is the answer.

I know it, it's still sitting deep.

You look at Sue across the pew, hair and nails always put together. Brand new car. Fresh tan from her latest vacation, diamond earrings the size of Texas. While you're nodding your head because this very situation is stirring memories, let me ask you two things:

1) Have you stopped to see the Christ shining through all those things?

2) Why are you so focused on Sue and not Jesus?

I know that just stung a little, but please, I need you to read this slowly and very carefully...

Sue does not have it all together.

Sue is looking at someone else wondering the exact same thing.

God has designed us all so very differently. There will only ever be one created to do the things God has set before you. Hold on to that.

You are so uniquely designed.

How amazing is that?!

Those stars that shine? He made you even more carefully than those.

The identity you are carrying, is the one destined before you were even a thought in the world. Know Abba made it with nothing but the most joyous love. It's the thumbprint He gave you, the one this world can never take away.

Those babies you hold while you scroll through Facebook and side eye Karen's latest vacation pics? God blessed you with those babies. He entrusted the ministry of caring for your sick mother. He hears those prayers full of grief when you pray for a husband who you aren't sure how to love anymore. The smallest of these task, are shouted about with delight in heaven.

God sees, He knows.

Your obedience and sacrifice does not go unnoticed.

Can I also give you a truth bomb?

Do you honestly think that if you had every shiny thing, everything your heart wanted, you would find peace in God? It's impossible to want the things of this world, and delight in the things God has given us.

～

"No one can serve two masters,

Either you will hate the one, and love the other,
or you will be devoted to one and despise the other.
You cannot serve both God and money."
Matthew 6:24

～

I need to tell you guys something. You will never find contentment, if you are not doing the things God has commissioned you with. Yes. That means, those babies at your feet, the husband you follow all over the world because his job says so. The battle with cancer that will be a testimony to carry someone else through.

Stop doubting God's great design, start remembering that the greatest thing ever given to you was the day the empty tomb was revealed. God longs to give us the things we crave, but those blessings also come with obedience. Another reality, those things you long for will change when you are walking in His service.

I am a wife and mother. All three of my guys have some kind of special need. The days it feels like a burden, are the days that I forget how I prayed for these boys, how I sought this husband He blessed me with. They are my "name in lights and shiney car" because God saw fit to give them to me. Every kiss, every hug,every stinky armpit I smell. Is because God trusted me with this task. When I lay in a hospital bed for 9 days because cancer had taken its toll on my body, this commissioned ministry was what carried me through.

So find ideas on Pinterest. Admire Sue's new shoes.

But remember God's gifts are far greater than anything you will ever find on this earth.

I look at my life right now, and this very moment I have contentment. I'm realizing these are all things I longed for, prayed for even as a little child. If you ask my mother, she will tell you, that one of my first wants was to be a wife and mother. But I spent so many years rebelling against that, because I let the world tell me who to be. How many moments, and memories did I lose sitting in discontentment?

I can even be honest and say in my teenage years I destroyed relationships and friendships trying to be someone who I wasn't. Lying, stealing, and spinning webs of deceit to be someone that God never planned for me. If you are in this cycle, please see the truth. God will forgive, simply ask. Know that whatever He ask you to put down, or walk away from He will restore. His will is always better than we can ever imagine. Don't suffer in your disobedience, Christ has done it for you already. Walk in His light Sis, walk in His truth.

Sparkle on,
Your (no-longer-pining-for-less) Sister in Christ
Denise

*S*tudy Questions

1. What are the things of this world that you put before God?
2. What is your plan to put them in their proper place?
3. How will you make an effort to pursue God more and delight in the gifts He has blessed you with?
4. Write down the longings of your heart and ask God to align those longings with His will.
5. Write a prayer of contentment. I'm going to give

you a little guidance here. The intimacy of prayer with a top so deep can be difficult.

Father God, in my heart, in your word, we know that the will you have for us is greater than we can ever imagine. Look in my heart Lord, reveal the things of unrest, things that are not pleasing to you. Help me seek and find the peace that comes with knowing that finding my worth, value, life longs are only fulfilled when seeking You first. Let me find joy in every season and circumstance. Remove the seeds of doubt the enemy has planted. Show me the beauty you have for my life. Amen.

'A SPOONFUL OF GRACE HELPS CURE THAT CASE OF THE GUILTS.'

"But whatever I am now, it is all because God poured out His special favor on me, and not without results. For I have worked harder than any other apostles; yet it was not I but God who was working through me by His grace." ~ 1 Corinthians 15:10

*D*ear Daughter seeking peace of mind,
   Have you ever just stood in the mirror and really looked at yourself? No makeup, no salon fresh hair. Was your first thought "I am beautifully, and wonderfully made"? It should have been, because you are.

You are going to have bad days. That baby of yours is going to have a meltdown in Target for no reason, you might just run around in mismatched shoes only to notice half way through the day, or that dinner you worked on for two hours is now on fire. Those days will happen, I guarantee it.

Take a deep breath and repeat after me...GUILT IS NOT FROM GOD. It absolute is NOT.

Will He correct, change your heart, and convict? Yes, double yes. There is a chasm of difference between conviction and guilt. Please do not forget that the enemy comes to kill, steal and destroy. Kill your dreams, steal your identity, and destroy any self worth you have stored in you. What better way than to make you feel that being nothing but a stay at home mom has no value. That because you had to lay down that dream of being a triathlete by 30 had to be put down. That you aren't anything more than the $10 Target shoes you're wearing.

You my beautiful friend, need to know it is okay to rest. It is okay to stay home and raise those babies, it is okay to take the job with less pay to make time for your ministry.

So, the dishes aren't done when your girlfriends drop by. To be honest, the ones who will fight with you, and for you, will not judge, but pick up the rag and help you start cleaning.

I still hold hard memories of a difficult season in my life. My husband was on his second deployment. We lived in Italy (I know poor pitiful me), I had a two year old, and a baby who had just turned six months. As my husband was leaving for Afghanistan, we were suspecting our 2 year old wasn't hitting milestones. Deep down my Momma heart knew, knew something was going on with our rainbow baby. This baby we had cried for, begged for, the one who was a blessing after so much loss. God you promised!!! And then I hear the gut punch word Autistic. I went inward, all the should of, would of...the things from my past. God is this my punishment?!

Then I heard God whisper to me sitting in that psychologist office. Felt His presence on my heart. "This boy is my promise. This boy will show you the true definition of love. This boy is mine. You will never be alone in the journey. Let my love and grace cover you. Nothing you have done would change this moment. Be still I AM is here."

I took a breath, and dove in with a fearless faith that can only come from GOD.

I could have let the guilt from the enemy soak over me in that moment. I could have believed his lies. I looked higher, I set my foundation on solid rock. I loved my boy. And when the enemy lets the worlds agenda slip in of who he should be, the guilt of not having a child who is "normal" by the world's standards. I shout back " He is a prince of the most High King, and was designed perfectly!"

I'm not going to lie to you. I struggle with guilt every day. But I long for the God convictions too. How do I know the difference? Because a conviction is a call to change. A moment of reflection. Knowing your will is not aligning with Gods. Something you are walking in, is not of His kingdom, is a stumbling block to you or others around you. Sound familiar?

" Lord we come to you, and ask You, remove those things we struggle with. Remove the ties of this world that bind. Remove the lies of the enemy that leave us feeling weighed down, unworthy, unloved. We proclaim they have no place in our hearts, minds, or homes. Show us what reflects gold in your eyes when you see us. Amen"

Something I always say to my boys in a teachable moment "Let someone who loves you correct you, before the world does."Wouldn't the correction of the one who loves you more than anyone be the ultimate goal? That correction holds no strings, and comes from a place of love, and from the one who designed you, who knows you better than you know yourself.

Conviction is correction from a place of love. Guilt is meant to tear you down, and leave you in a place of unworthiness and shame.

Quick note here....Let's stop doing this to one another. Lets stop tearing down the ones we need to build up. Lets stop making a teachable moment of love, become one of judgment. Do not condemn others in their walk. You too where once there. Let's get back to a place of biblical fellowship, in stewarding relationships that are modeled in Titus. Correct in love, not condemnation. Did you check the log in your eye before you spoke on it?

I've learned over the last few years, I never want to stop being teachable, not only by God, but by those who have come before me. I want the words of the disciples to be my truth when walking this life. I want the wisdom of those I encounter every day to be scales of conviction, and that the weight of condemnation to stay right at satan's feet where it belongs.

～

" A new command I give you: Love one another. As I have loved you, so you must love one another. By this everyone will know that you are my disciples, if you love one another." ~ John 14:34-35

28

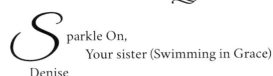

*S*parkle On,
        Your sister (Swimming in Grace)
Denise

*S*tudy Questions:

1. Write down at least 3 things you struggle with. Now cross them out. Write out a prayer, asking God to show you the convictions in these areas. Note: Don't be surprised if the conviction is dropping the guilt.
2. Write down a time where you felt the presence of God in a moment of conviction.
3. How is identifying guilt vs. conviction a blessing?
4. Read in your bible John 8:1-11. Notice how Jesus handled those condemning (guilt)? How did he handle the women in sin? Note the last verse: "Neither do I condemn you, go and sin no more."

'I'VE GOT A PURPOSE, YOU'VE GOT A
PURPOSE, AND SHE'S GOT A
PURPOSE. WE'VE ALL GOT A
PURPOSE!!!'

*"Commit your actions to the Lord, and your plans will
succeed."~ Proverbs 16:3*

*D*ear Daughter trying to figure out the meaning of
life,
If you had told me at 18 that I would be a stay at home

Army wife, following a man all over the world every 2-3 year, I would have laughed in your face hysterically. Admittedly, for the first six years of my marriage I selfishly struggled. This was not the white picket fence and the 2.5 kids and two matching chocolate labs I had envisioned! The defining moment was when I begged God to show me my purpose. When I let the "what about me" go, and surrendered my will to Him.

I'm about to tell ya'll another little secret here...The very moment I realized that God's will was greater than mine, I realized my purpose, my passions. He blessed me with have always been apparent, and I couldn't be blessed with a better life. My God ordained life.

I'm sure if you're looking at this, you're thinking 'Denise, doesn't this fit right in with "Embrace who God made you chapter?" Well yes, and no. Understanding your identity, and knowing that we all have a purpose in this world, and more specifically God's Kingdom go hand and hand.

A few things to think about and hold onto here:

1. Although at times we maybe serving in the same area, same ministry, our purpose is different, God's design for us in these situations is different.
2. Do not compare your purpose with someone else's. Just like all thumbprints are different, so is our purpose. No two will be the same.
3. The roles we play, the obedience we step forward in are always going to be inline with the great commission, to lift God's Kingdom, serve and find those who are lost and seeking salvation.

I know, I just threw a lot of deep thought at you. So let me give you some ideas to chew on here. Let's say you are in a season of life where you have raised your kids. Maybe God is calling you to a Titus/mentorship situation. God will lead you to people. Maybe these people are going through struggles, you have faced. Maybe they just need a genuine listening ear, and help in areas of life and walking in faith. Either way no two situations will be the same. God will call you into these people's lives for a reason. These relationship maybe for a season, a lifetime, but know it is for a reason. And also know just maybe you may never know the end result until you embrace again in heaven. You were the purpose in that moment.

I'm at blissful year 37 of life. It looks nothing like year 27. At 27, I was able to walk a path of being the auntie by association for so many military babies. I was blessed to be the relief when Mom had too many babies, not enough hands or sleep, and Dad was on the mission field. I was in the pickup line, caring for toddlers who weren't mine so mom could finish her degree. I was the reason, that was my purpose.

In those 10 years that have passed since then, many times I've been blessed to be someone's purpose. I've been the awkward rewalking in faith that someone embraced and showed how to walk in biblical womanhood. I've been the one to lay down my pride, and let others be my hands and feet when recovering from biopsies and cancer treatments. I've been the one (too many necessary times) to be corrected in love.

Honey, let me tell you something, even if your daily task is currently wiping butts, or cleaning up after unappreciative people. It is a purpose. There is always an opportunity to shine God's light in every moment.

"Then the King will say to those on His right, 'Come, you who are blessed by my Father; take your inheritance, the kingdom

prepared for you since the creation of the world. For I was hungry and you gave me something to eat, I was thirsty and you gave me something to drink, I was a stranger and you invited me in, I needed clothes and you clothed me, I was sick and you looked after me, I was in prison and you came to visit me." ~Matthew 25:34-36

≈

*D*on't doubt how God will use you. Me writing this book, sharing my heart for Jesus. Was spoken to me over fourteen years ago, by a housekeeper. Who sent me back into God's arms. Who God gave wisdom too. Who knew my life's journey would need His light. Who is forever now a sister in Christ.

Your purpose has passion. Let it be God's passion that fuels you. Know that in the purpose you will find struggles. But the things you labor in do not go unnoticed. Do not go without praise.

Baby you've got a purpose! Let your soul be set on fire by the purpose God has given you.

*S*parkle On,
    Your sister (owning her purpose like a shiny unicorn)
    Denise

≈

*S*tudy Questions:

1. Write down some strengths. How can you use those things as a purpose?

2. Has there been a time in your life, where someone's purpose has blessed you?
3. Have you asked God to shine a light on your purpose? Write it down, make it a prayer.
4. What are somethings in your life that you know are your purpose?

'HONEY, GET YOURSELF A VILLAGE.'

"Jesus replied, you must love the Lord your God with all your heart, all your soul, and all your mind. This is the first and greatest commandment. Second is equally important: love your neighbor as yourself. The entire las and all the demands of the prophets are based on these two commandments." ~Matthew 22:37-40

*D*ear Daughter feeling lost and alone,
         Repeat after me, "I cannot do it all on my own,
just because I need help, does not make me weak". One of the
biggest lies Satan will tell you, is that we don't need anyone.
He wants you isolated, feeling alone, and vulnerable. From
the beginning of creation God created companionship.

I would have not made it to this very moment without my
village. I feel I'm even more blessed because my village runs
far and deep. Things I felt I would lose becoming an army
wife and living a nomadic life, has definitely become a true
definition of sisterhood.

Do not, I repeat, DO NOT hold a predisposition for what
your village will look like.

Do embrace the misfits, the lost, the lonely, the shy kid in
the corner. We are reminded over in over in the New Testa-
ment, how Jesus sat with and called the unlikely. You know
why? Because those are the ones who have the most love to
give, have no shame and declaring, "I'm lost and broken too!
I need Jesus too! So, let's do this mess we call life together!"

So how do you find that village. You pray for one, you
leave the judgment behind. Take joy when you look around
and know that without Jesus none of you would have ever
become friends.

My village is a rainbow of women across a range of
ethnic and economic backgrounds, all baring scars, and
weights from this world. My village is my rainbow of promise. My village.... brings tears of joy at just the thought of it.

Here's the kicker, what if I told you my village included
drug addicts, prostitutes, thieves, those not quiet walking
with Jesus, liars, single moms, divorcees, adulterers, and I
love the mess out of every single one of them. I love them all
because God ordained these relationships long ago. I walk
with them, I love them. Why....because we are all saints who

are sinners. Not sinners trying to become saints. Sin, is sin in the eyes of God. If I judge my village the way the world tells me to for their past transgressions, I would be a sad lonely sap sitting in my house still believing my sins and past define me. I would walk around with blinders of judgement, would have failed in my walk, in my rescue, in thriving and not just surviving this life.

My village teaches me humility, my village teaches me to laugh, love without judgment, to humble myself, to straighten my crown. My village loves me because of who Christ created, not because of what I can do for them.

If you are part of a village who isn't lifting you up, who isn't reminding you to pray, who doesn't rejoice in your wins, and mourns with you in your losses....BABY....get a new village.

Should we surround ourselves with like believers, why yes of course. But I take pride that no two people in my village have the same background. Heck some of us could find ourselves on opposite sides of the line when it comes to politics, and church experiences. But the common denominator of Jesus is what drives the love we have for one another.

Much in the way the world judged Jesus for who He broke bread with, I want the world to do the same to me. Because that means I'm following in His truth. I want a Mary Magdelend, I want a doubting Thomas, I want a Paul. Through Gods love, patience and understanding, they became glitter from ashes.

Sparkle On,
Your sister (Wrapped in a Village of love)
Denise

∼

tudy Questions:

1. What are somethings that stand out to you about your current village/friendships while reading this chapter. Positive or negative?
2. Are you purposeful in your relationships?
3. Take the time to write out a prayer for two members of your village that are currently struggling. Spend the next week praying for them every day.
4. Are you being the best villager possible? Are there areas where you could strengthen your friendships?
5. How does the thought of a strong village empower you to spread the great commission?

'RECHARGE, RENEW.'

"Create in me a clean heart. O God. Renew a loyal spirit within me." ~Psalm 51:10

*D*ear Daughter feeling exhausted and frustrated,
    It is by nature as women, that we put others first, and ourselves all too often dead last. We pour and pour

into others. Leaving our cup dry. We say yes without thinking. Let self-doubt, or our need to be accepted or needed take over. Then we find ourselves at the brink of a meltdown, reheating that cup of coffee for the 8th time, and realizing that strange smell is in fact coming from the body you've neglected to bathe over the last three days.

Let me paint this picture for you:

There is a church/bible study member in need. You signed up to bring a meal, because that's what we do right?! But you forgot that day. So now you're running 90 to nothing through the grocery store before you head to get the kids. Praying you didn't forget something. Now you're home cooking and hustling trying to get out the door on time to deliver said meal. You're yelling at your tiny blessings, saying not so kind things as you trip over the dog on the way out the door. Deliver the meal. Yes! And then pull into the nearest drive through to feed your family....see what just happened there?

There was no Joy in that? Did you even have time to stop and truly chat with the meal recipient? Pray with them, ask what maybe they needed besides that rushed meal. Now you're frustrated and regretting those cold french fries.

I'm about to give ya'll two very powerful tools to use:

The word NO

A calendar with blocked off days for purposeful rest.

Need even more biblical backing in this? Jesus rested. We see several times in scripture where He left to pray, to rest, to get away from it all. What makes us think we are better than that. That we can still run on fumes and be successful in this thing called life.

～

"Very early in the morning, while it was still dark, Jesus got up, left

the house, and went off to a solitary place, where He prayed."
~Mark 1:35

"After Jesus had dismissed the crowds, He went up on a
mountainside by Himself to pray. When evening came, He was still
there alone."~ Mark 6:31-32

⤳

*H*ere where some relations hit home for me. We have got to be okay with spending alone time with ourselves. We have got to leave the noise and chaos of the world go sometimes to recharge with the peace and presence of the Holy Spirit.

The world will constantly demand from us, take from us, use up all we have to give till our well is dry. And you know what? They will move right on to the next person. Even in matters of serving others, we must set boundaries.

Has God given you talents and blessing to share? I know He has, but what's the point when it all becomes a matter of stress and frustration. Do you pray before you give the Yes, especially in matters of your time, and how it lines up to your other ministries.

The longer you run ragged in these things, the easier you have left the door open for the chaos of the enemy to walk in. Yelling at your spouse more often? Kids driving you crazy, the tiniest thing setting you off? Now you're restless and aren't sleeping well at night. Relating to the word "triggered" seems more of a likelihood. Now your sick for the third time this month, and wait..what happened to the Joy you once found in the simplest of things?

Rest. Renew. Reset.

Don't let that whisper from the enemy have you believing that day of doing nothing is laziness. Honey, I promise that dirty laundry will be there later, and your kids won't suffer if they have to eat leftovers. Those 500 hundred emails, the girlfriends who just want to blow steam with idle chit chat, it can all wait. It will be there. It's not worth your piece of mind. Not worth your health, not worth your relationship with God to work yourself into a broken shell. That is not what God intended when He instructed it us with the great commission. He rested, He gave us Sabbath.

Another thought here, why are you working yourself to the bone? Are you running from something, trying to stay busy so you don't have to think about that hurt, situation, or person. Let me hand you a glitter bomb....It ain't going to work. When you finally crash from the weariness, it's all still going to be there.

Sit, rest, lay it at the cross.

Renew, refresh, remember who you were designed to be.

Those gifts and talents will still be there. If you need a great alternative to No, simply say, "Let me think on it, pray about. And i'll let you know." Sometimes a situation warrants that any way.

Nothing in this world is worth being removed from the peace of God. Nothing. Not our ministries, jobs, friendships, money...NOTHING.

Step away, go up on that mountain, have time with yourself and God.

"Peace I leave with you; my peace I give you. I do not give to you as the world gives. Do not let your hearts be troubled and do not be afraid." ~John 14:27

Sparkle on,

Your sister (Napping like it's an olympic event)

Denise

tudy Questions:

1. What are some things that make you feel that you can not find time to rest?
2. Look at your daily/weekly schedule, are you stretching yourself thin? Where can you make time for rest, and spiritual renewal?
3. Do you pray before you say, "yes,"to things? How can you make this a better practice.
4. Why do you think Jesus took the time to rest?

'FAITH, FAMILY, THEN EVERYTHING ELSE.'

Yes, I am the vine; you are the branches. Those who remain in me, and I in them, will produce much fruit. For a part from me you can do nothing."~ Matthew 15:5

*D*ear Daughter balancing it all,

For so long, the thought of loving anyone more than my husband, or myself for that matter, was utterly insane to me. I would laugh it off, give the person saying such nonsense the stank eye, or just write it off all together. And then in a moment of earth shattering despair, the ugly crying while hiding in the dark moment, I heard Him. "Dear daughter, it hurts me to see you this way, please give me your trust, I will never fail you, I am here, I will always be here. Seek me always, and I will fill the void." It was that simple. From that moment forward, if my life doesn't line up this way, it a stinky hot mess.

God

Myself

My Husband/Relationship

My children

Everything Else

God because in the simplest of terms, I owe it all to Him. He is my Alpha and Omega, the beginning and the end to all that moves my world. The well that never runs dry. Wisdom, comfort, knowledge beyond measure. Way maker, unfailing love. Even simpler this is one of the very first things He asks of us. If you aren't focused on Him, it will fall apart.

"But seek God first His kingdom, His righteousness, and all these things will be given to you as well." ~Matthew 6:33

~

*S*eek Him and find peace. Seek Him and find balance. Seek Him and lack for nothing. Seek Him and the things of this world will not matter. Seek Him and His will be done.

Myself, because others can not pull from a dry well. Did we not just cover this? How you going to run that household, move mountains with that ministry, give of yourself in courages ways for the kingdom, heck put food on the table and keep the tiny humans alive, if you can't even with your own self.

If you can not look at the beautiful being that is you, if you can not see the love that you were created with, then seek God again my friend. Because this is part of the armor you will need to make it on God's terms, not the worlds.

" I have been crucified with Christ and I no longer live, but Christ lives in me. The life I now live in the body, I live by faith in the Son of God, who love me and gave Himself for me."~Galatians 2:20

My husband. This man was given to me by God. He is my partner, my help mate. My other half. I can feel his presence before he is even in the same building as me. He is my song of Solomon. Why would I not confide in him. My KJ is the one I seek when I need advice, he is the leader of our home. I trust him with my life. I made a covenant to nurture our relationship, to stick it out no matter the mountain. And let me tell you, in the 15 years of being blessed with my honey, there have been mountain's. I've not always done right by him. But God! Gods grace through it all. When the kids grow old, and seasons of friendships fall away. I am my lovers and my lover is mine.

*"There are three things that are too amazing for me, four that I do
not understand; the way of an eagle in the sky, the way of a snake
on a rock, the way of a ship on the high seas, and the way of a man
with a woman." ~ Proverbs 30:18-19*

$\sim$

*M*y children. My handsome little humans. The
ones whose farts and armpit smells I'm sure
to miss in the days to come. Life as a Momma is frustrating.
There is no denying that raising another human being is one
of the hardest, most rewarding, tear jerking, loveable, hold
your tongue task that God ever created. And before I go a
little deeper, let me stop a second to recognize you coura-
geous brave women, who struggle to have babies, who have
lost children, who are on the journey to adopt, or who have
simply decided that raising children is not your thing. I see
you Ma'. I see you. I see the greatness in you. God sees you.

Parenthood is a blessing. My children are my first
prospect of the great commission. I can only imagine the Joy
God has for us as He watches us interact with His blessings
to us. My first true glimpse of this was listening to my
youngest son accept Christ into his little 4 year old heart. I
thought in that moment, "Lord this is the joy you feel, the
pride you feel, when we come to you." Why would I not make
this a priority over everything else.

"Listen, my son, to your father's instruction and do not
forsake your mother's teaching. They are a garland to grace
your head and a chain to adorn your neck." Proverbs 1:8-9

Everything else...Y'all it's just that simple. You have to
prioritize the things that are important. When God is at the
top of that list, it is that simple. I've been blessed to lead
women's ministry groups, speak to groups and crowds of

people, work with Chaplain's who are at the forefront of the war's this country wages in. But you know what? When those things become a priority, when number 1 becomes number 8, and my eyes slip off God. The chaos slips in, and I'm left feeling weary and at a loss as to how I got there. There will be seasons that you are busy, you will be called to do things in life that will have you shifting and rescheduling, but do not forget that priority list, and do not forget who needs to sit at the top of it. Stay grounded to Him. Stay humble. The only thing in this life that should sit on any kind of pedestal is God the Father. Can I get an AMEN!

"The Kingdom of heaven is like treasure hidden in a field. When a man found it, he hid it again, and then in his joy went and sold all he had and bought that field. Again, the kingdom of heaven is like a merchant looking for pearls. When he found one of great value, he went away and sold everything he had and bought it." ~ Matthew 13:44-46

Let Him reign in your life. There will never be a moment you will regret doing this. Have that faith to sell it all and buy the field, Gods got you. You just gotta put Him at the top of it all. Recognize and cherish the things He puts in your life. God, then everything else.

Sparkle On,

Your sister(Seeking God first)

Denise

*S*tudy Questions:

1. If you looked at a list of things that you consider priority in life, where does God sit on that list?
2. What value do you see in putting God first in all you do?

3. What things in life cause you not to put God first?
4. What are some changes you can make to put God back at the top of your list?
5. Write your priority list out, write a prayer next to each thing you find a priority.

YOUR CHAPTER... THE START OF YOUR SPARKLE

"God said, to Moses "I AM WHO I AM", and he said, "Thus you shall say to the sons of Israel, 'I AM has sent me to you."
~Exodus 3:14

So here we are. At the end of this journey together. I'm going to share with you guys it has taken me 2 years to be able to finish this ministry God placed on my heart to share with you. As I wrote these pages to you, I moved states and house three times. I walked with my husband as he laid down a 14 year career as a soldier to learn how to become "normal" again. I've laid in a hospital bed dying for 9 days. I've held my youngest child as anxiety and panic gripped his body to the point where he no longer knew how to function. I've been lied on, stabbed in the back by those I trusted, and wrestled with the demons of suicide and depression.

But. GOD. OUR MIGHTY GOD.

He gave me platforms to share my truth, and His glory. He gave me peace to surpass all understanding when I laid in the hospital bed. He gave us a village to carry us through a transition in life we never saw coming when my husband was no longer called sergeant. He sent prayer worries to cover my family when the enemy was beating down our door. He kept His promise.

Those foundation cracks were sealed with His love. I found my purpose. I made Him and my family a priority. I learned that turning up the worship music when I don't feel Gods presence is the best way to confuse the enemy. I spent hours in my prayer chair pouring over scripture and praying for others. I found my crown, and get such joy in straightening others. I let God define my beauty when I look in the mirror.

I share this so that you know that you can come to Jesus in any season. Don't think you have to get to a certain place to approach the throne of God. He will leave the 99 for you. Let people see Him shine in you.

Start this moment, in this blank space I'm leave you. Make it your own. Find that sparkle that God gave you. Shield your heart from the world, shine your armor and know that hope starts when you call out the name of Jesus.

Take that Holy Spirit dwelling in you, and GO SHINE!

THANK YOU . . .

I can not let this book end without thanking so many amazing people in my life.

Mr. Glitter aka Kenton Jolly, Thank you my love. Thank you for all the adventures. Thank you for fueling all the cupcakes and coffee. I love the heart you have for Jesus. The way you love me and our boys. Thank you for loving me through all these seasons, and pouring my heart into this book. God made you for me.

Morgan Farr, you are amazing. You are have been such a tremendous part of my journey. Thank you for putting up with all the ramblings. Pouring over this book, and making sure it was readable. You my sweet sister are an amazing testimony to God's love. I will forever be grateful that God brought us together.

Nicole Dunlap. Books brought us together, but God's love made you my sister. Thank you for not letting me give up on my dream. Thank you for believing in me.

Tia LaRue, you are magic behind a camera. Thank you for capturing these beauty images for this book.

Thank you and so much love for Lighthouse Coffee in Lake Carolina, South Carolina. This amazing Christ filled coffee shop was just what I needed to make this book happen. Thank you for all the coffee, yummy treats and love. Most importantly thank you for creating a place where Gods light and glory shines.

Looking for more Glitter in your life?! Find me on social media:

The Glitter From Ashes - The Glitter From Ashes Blog
  The Glitter from Ashes - Home | Facebook

Made in the USA
Columbia, SC
16 February 2020